by Iain Gray

PUBLISHING

WRITING *to* REMEMBER

LangSyne

PUBLISHING

WRITING *to* REMEMBER

79 Main Street, Newtongrange,
Midlothian EH22 4NA
Tel: 0131 344 0414   Fax: 0845 075 6085
E-mail: info@lang-syne.co.uk
www.langsyneshop.co.uk

Design by Dorothy Meikle
Printed by Printwell Ltd
© Lang Syne Publishers Ltd 2018

ISBN 978-1-85217-589-4

Jones

MOTTO:
Without God, without anything.

CREST:
A lion rampant.

NAME variations include:
Jonas
Jone
Joness

Chapter one:

The origins of popular surnames

by George Forbes and Iain Gray

If you don't know where you came from, you won't know where you're going is a frequently quoted observation and one that has a particular resonance today when there has been a marked upsurge in interest in genealogy, with increasing numbers of people curious to trace their family roots.

Main sources for genealogical research include census returns and official records of births, marriages and deaths – and the key to unlocking the detail they contain is obviously a family surname, one that has been 'inherited' and passed from generation to generation.

No matter our station in life, we all have a surname – but it was not until about the middle of the fourteenth century that the practice of being identified by a particular surname became commonly established throughout the British Isles.

Previous to this, it was normal for a person to be identified through the use of only a forename.

But as population gradually increased and there were many more people with the same forename, surnames were adopted to distinguish one person, or community, from another.

Many common English surnames are patronymic in origin, meaning they stem from the forename of one's father – with 'Johnson,' for example, indicating 'son of John.'

It was the Normans, in the wake of their eleventh century conquest of Anglo-Saxon England, a pivotal moment in the nation's history, who first brought surnames into usage – although it was a gradual process.

For the Normans, these were names initially based on the title of their estates, local villages and chateaux in France to distinguish and identify these landholdings.

Such grand descriptions also helped enhance the prestige of these warlords and generally glorify their lofty positions high above the humble serfs slaving away below in the pecking order who had only single names, often with Biblical connotations as in Pierre and Jacques.

The only descriptive distinctions among the peasantry concerned their occupations, like 'Pierre the swineherd' or 'Jacques the ferryman.'

Roots of surnames that came into usage in England not only included Norman-French, but also Old French, Old Norse, Old English, Middle English, German, Latin, Greek, Hebrew and the Gaelic languages of the Celts.

The Normans themselves were originally Vikings, or 'Northmen', who raided, colonised and eventually settled down around the French coastline.

The had sailed up the Seine in their longboats in 900AD under their ferocious leader Rollo and ruled the roost in north eastern France before sailing over to conquer England in 1066 under Duke William of Normandy – better known to posterity as William the Conqueror, or King William I of England.

Granted lands in the newly-conquered England, some of their descendants later acquired territories in Wales, Scotland and Ireland – taking not only their own surnames, but also the practice of adopting a surname, with them.

But it was in England where Norman rule and custom first impacted, particularly in relation to the adoption of surnames.

This is reflected in the famous *Domesday Book*, a massive survey of much of England and Wales, ordered by William I, to determine who owned what, what it was worth and therefore how much they were liable to pay in taxes to the voracious Royal Exchequer.

Completed in 1086 and now held in the National Archives in Kew, London, 'Domesday' was an Old English word meaning 'Day of Judgement.'

This was because, in the words of one contemporary chronicler, "its decisions, like those of the Last Judgement, are unalterable."

It had been a requirement of all those English landholders – from the richest to the poorest – that they identify themselves for the purposes of the survey and for future reference by means of a surname.

This is why the *Domesday Book*, although written in Latin as was the practice for several centuries with both civic and ecclesiastical records, is an invaluable source for the early appearance of a wide range of English surnames.

Several of these names were coined in connection with occupations.

These include Baker and Smith, while Cooks, Chamberlains, Constables and Porters were to be found carrying out duties in large medieval households.

The church's influence can be found in names such as Bishop, Friar and Monk while the popular name of Bennett derives from the late fifth to mid-sixth century Saint Benedict, founder of the Benedictine order of monks.

The early medical profession is represented by Barber, while businessmen produced names that include Merchant and Sellers.

Down at the village watermill, the names that cropped up included Millar/Miller, Walker and Fuller, while other self-explanatory trades included Cooper, Tailor, Mason and Wright.

Even the scenery was utilised as in Moor, Hill, Wood and Forrest – while the hunt and the chase supplied names that include Hunter, Falconer, Fowler and Fox.

Colours are also a source of popular surnames, as in Black, Brown, Gray/Grey, Green and White, and would have denoted the colour of the clothing the person habitually wore or, apart from the obvious exception of 'Green', one's hair colouring or even complexion.

The surname Red developed into Reid, while

Blue was rare and no-one wanted to be associated with yellow.

Rather self-important individuals took surnames that include Goodman and Wiseman, while physical attributes crept into surnames such as Small and Little.

Many families proudly boast the heraldic device known as a Coat of Arms, as featured on our front cover.

The central motif of the Coat of Arms would originally have been what was borne on the shield of a warrior to distinguish himself from others on the battlefield.

Not featured on the Coat of Arms, but high-lighted on page three, is the family motto and related crest – with the latter frequently different from the central motif.

Adding further variety to the rich cultural heritage that is represented by surnames is the appearance in recent times in lists of the 100 most common names found in England of ones that include Khan, Patel and Singh – names that have proud roots in the vast sub-continent of India.

Echoes of a far distant past can still be found in our surnames and they can be borne with pride in commemoration of our forebears.

Chapter two:

Fields of battle

The most common name in Wales and the second most common in England, 'Jones' means 'son of John', while in Wales it derives from 'Ioan', 'Ieuan' or 'Sion', all Welsh versions of 'John'.

The name John, in turn, derives from the Latin personal name 'Johannes', meaning 'Yahweh is gracious' – and with 'Yahweh' indicating 'God', that is why Jones is a name with truly religious connotations.

This may explain the Jones motto of 'Without God, without anything' – an English translation of the original Welsh 'Heb dduw, heb ddim'.

'Jones' is recorded in the English county of Huntingdonshire as early as 1279, but even earlier in the Denbighshire area of Northeast Wales, where one prominent family of the name had a seat at Llanerchrugog.

Flowing through the veins of some bearers of the name today may well be the blood of the ancient Britons. Of Celtic pedigree, these early inhabitants of the British Isles were settled for centuries from a line south of the River Forth in Scotland all the way down to the south coast of England and with a particular presence in Wales.

Speaking a Celtic language known as Brythonic, they boasted a glorious culture that flourished even after the Roman invasion of Britain in 43 AD and the subsequent consolidation of Roman power by about 84 AD.

With many of the original Britons absorbing aspects of Roman culture, they became 'Romano-British' – while still retaining their own proud Celtic heritage.

Following the withdrawal of the last Roman legions from Britain in 406, what is now modern-day Wales, or *Cymru*, fragmented into a number of independent kingdoms – with the most powerful king being recognised as overall ruler.

Meanwhile, with the motto of 'Cymru am byth', ('Wales Forever'), this early homeland of those who would come to bear the Jones name was annexed to the English Crown in 1284 and it is from this date that the heir apparent to the British throne has borne the title of Prince of Wales.

A bloody rebellion erupted in 1294, when England's Edward I imperiously ordered the conscription to his armed ranks of the famed Welsh longbow men, to help him in his territorial battles with France's Philip IV.

A national leader arose in the form of Madog ap Llywelyn of Merioneth, who inflicted a number of stunning defeats on the English army that had occupied Wales. But the short-lived rebellion was brutally crushed in March of the following year and the nation subjugated.

An abortive rebellion was led in the early fifteenth century by the freedom fighter Owain Glyndŵr, while in the following century, under Henry VIII, Wales was 'incorporated' into the English kingdom.

In 1707, in common with Scotland, Wales became incorporated into the United Kingdom. It was not until 1998 that the Welsh were granted devolved governing powers through the creation of the National Assembly for Wales, based in Cardiff.

Bearers of the Jones name figure prominently in the historical record of not only Wales in particular but also that of the United Kingdom in general.

During the seventeenth century English Civil War, Philip Jones, born in Swansea in 1618, fought with the rank of colonel in the Parliamentary Army.

The monarch Charles I had incurred the wrath of Parliament by his insistence on the 'divine right' of monarchs, and added to this was Parliament's fear of Catholic 'subversion' against the state and the king's stubborn refusal to grant demands for religious and constitutional concessions.

Matters came to a head with the outbreak of the Civil War in 1642, with Parliamentary forces, known as the New Model Army and commanded by Oliver Cromwell and Sir Thomas Fairfax, arrayed against the Royalist army of the king.

In what became an increasingly bloody and complex conflict, spreading to Scotland and Ireland and with rapidly shifting loyalties on both sides, the 49-year-old king was eventually captured and executed in January of 1649 on the orders of Parliament.

As governor of Swansea in the early stages of the war, Philip Jones successfully defended it against Royalist forces, while in 1649 he was appointed governor of Cardiff. Elected a year later as Member of Parliament (MP) for Breconshire and later as MP for Monmouthshire, he also served for a time as MP for Glamorgan.

Appointed a Privy Councillor and also comptroller of Oliver Cromwell – known as 'The Great Protector' – he officiated at his state funeral following his death in November of 1658.

His high office enabled him to accrue vast wealth, not least through the acquisition of lands forfeited by Royalists or bought from them at knock-down prices. In common with many other prominent Parliamentarians – excluding those who had signed Charles I's death warrant – he managed to seek an accommodation with the new Royalist regime following the Restoration of Charles II in 1660.

Appointed High Sheriff of Glamorgan in 1671, he died three years later in Fonmon Castle, in the Vale of Glamorgan which he had bought in 1654 from the St John family. The castle, owned by Sir Brook Boothby, one of his descendants, is now a popular events and wedding venue.

In a much different and later conflict, part of which was fought on the high seas, John Paul Jones was the naval commander and hero of the American War of Independence of 1775 to 1783.

Born in 1747 on the Arbigland estate near Kirkbean, in the Stewarty of Kircudbright, on the southern coast of Scotland, this son of a humble gardener was destined to become recognised as 'Father of the American Navy', thanks to his daring naval exploits on behalf of his adopted country.

He first went to sea at the age of 13, sailing

out of the northern English port of Whitehaven, later serving aboard a number of merchant ships and steadily rising through the ranks of command.

But, facing trial in 1772 for killing one of his crew in a dispute over wages, he fled to Fredericksburg, in Virginia, where his older brother who had settled there some years earlier had recently died.

It was some time after this that he adopted the name 'Jones' as his surname, having actually been born John Paul. This was in honour of his friend the statesman Willie Jones, of Halifax, North Carolina, who had inspired him with his revolutionary views, and for whom present day Jones County in North Carolina is named.

On the outbreak of the American War of Independence, also known as the American Revolutionary War, Jones offered his services to the newly-established Continental Navy, soon to become known as the United States Navy, and was assigned the rank of 1st Lieutenant.

A number of successful engagements against the British Navy followed, and on June 14, 1777, the memorable day on which the flag known as the Stars and Stripes was first adopted, he was given command of the fighting vessel *Ranger*.

Less than a year later, revolutionary France was in alliance with America, and it was from the French port of Brest that Captain John Paul Jones sailed in April of 1778 to launch attacks on the western coast of Britain – most notably an assault on Whitehaven, the very port from which as a young lad he had embarked on his career at sea.

In August of the following year, in command of the *Bonhomme Richard* and in a furious engagement with the British Navy off Flamborough Head, Jones uttered his famous "I have not yet begun to fight!" when the tide of battle appeared to be turning against him.

Following the conclusion of the war in 1783, Jones found service with the Russian Navy for a time, eventually dying in Paris in July of 1792 showered with honours from America, France and Russia.

He was buried in the French capital, but his body was returned to America with great ceremony in 1906 and later re-interred in a bronze and marble sarcophagus in the Naval Academy Chapel in Annapolis.

In his original homeland, the cottage in which he was born on the Arbigland estate was restored in 1993 and houses a museum dedicated to the famous seafarer's colourful life and times.

Chapter three:

Honours and fame

From the high seas to the world of architecture, Inigo Jones, born in the Smithfield area of London in 1573, was the renowned architect responsible for some of the capital's earliest and most famous landmarks.

The son of a cloth-maker, surprisingly little is known of his early life despite a fame that has endured to this day, but what is known is that it was when he was aged about 25 that he made the first of two visits to Italy to study its magnificent Renaissance architecture.

Inspired by what he saw and studied, he returned to his native land and over the next few decades introduced the Renaissance style to the city of his birth. Most notable examples of this are the Queen's House, at Greenwich, which he started in 1616, the Banqueting House at Whitehall and the design of Covent Garden.

In addition to his work as an architect, Jones also turned his talents to stage design, working with such great English playwrights as Ben Jonson.

As Surveyor of Works to King Charles I,

Jones, who died in 1652, also conducted the first detailed survey of the ancient group of standing stones in Wiltshire known as Stonehenge. It was his detailed measurements of the mysterious Neolithic site that revealed how it had been laid out with meticulous mathematical precision, leading future scholars to speculate that this may have been in order to align it with the movements of the sun and the moon.

Returning to the battlefield, Robert Digby-Jones was a posthumous Scottish recipient of the Victoria Cross, the highest award for bravery in the face of enemy action for British and Commonwealth forces.

Born in 1876 in Edinburgh, he was a lieutenant in the Corps of Royal Engineers during the South African War, also known as the Boer War, when, in January of 1900, during an attack on Wagon Hill, at Ladysmith, he and a trooper of the Imperial Light Horse led a force which managed to re-occupy the hill after Jones shot the enemy leader dead before he was also shot and killed.

His Victoria Cross is displayed at the Royal Engineers Museum in Chatham, England.

In more contemporary times, Lieutenant Colonel Herbert Jones, who was more familiarly known as 'H' Jones, was another posthumous recipient of the Victoria Cross. Born in Putney in 1940, he was commanding officer of 2nd Battalion, Parachute Regiment, during Britain's war with Argentina known as the Falklands War, when, on May 28, 1982, he led an attack on enemy positions in an around the settlements of Darwin and Goose Green. He was killed after seizing a machine-gun and single-handedly launching a charge on the enemy trenches.

In an earlier conflict, that of the Second World War, Professor Reginald Victor Jones, better known as Professor R.V. Jones, was the English physicist and expert in scientific military intelligence who is recognised as having played a vital role in Britain's defence.

Born in 1911, he served as assistant director of intelligence (science) to Britain's Air Ministry, and it was in this role that he helped to develop technologies that include 'chaff' – strips of aluminium foil dropped from aircraft to confuse enemy radar.

Known today as 'the father of scientific and technical intelligence', in 1993 he became the first recipient of the R.V. Jones Intelligence Award, created in his honour by America's CIA.

Author of *Most Secret War: British Scientific Intelligence 1939-45*, he died in 1997.

From heroes of warfare to heroes of a rather different order, John Luther Jones, born in 1863, was the American railroad engineer better known as Casey Jones.

Employed by the Illinois Central Railroad, it had been on a rainy and foggy night in April of 1900, as his passenger train approached Vaughan, in Mississippi, that he and his fellow engine crew realised they were in danger of colliding with a stalled freight train. The rest of the crew jumped overboard, but Casey remained to apply the brakes and lessen the force of the impact, as a result of which no one was killed or seriously injured.

All, that is, apart from Casey Jones himself, whose dead body was pulled from the twisted wreckage with his hand still clutched to the brake.

It was his friend and fellow railroad worker Wallace Saunders who later immortalised his brave actions in the popular *Ballad of Casey Jones*.

In the often cut-throat worlds of business and politics, Digby Marritt Jones, better known as Digby Jones and more formally as Digby, Lord Jones of Birmingham, served as director general of the Confederation of British Industry (CBI) from 2000 to 2006.

Born in Birmingham in 1955, a graduate in law from University College, London and a former sub-lieutenant in the Royal Navy, he also served from 2007 to 2008 as Minister of State for Trade and Investment.

Knighted in 2005 and elevated to the Peerage as Lord Jones in 2007, his many business interests include chairmanship of Triumph Motorcycles Ltd; and corporate ambassador for Jaguar cars, while he is also a business ambassador at UK Trade and Investment.

One particularly infamous bearer of the otherwise proud name of Jones was Harold Jones, the Welsh child killer born in 1906 in Abertillery, South Wales. He was aged 15 when he was acquitted at Monmouth Assizes for the brutal murder of an eight-year-old girl in his home town. Only a few weeks later, however, he murdered an eleven-year-old girl – a crime to which he confessed in addition to finally admitting he had also killed the eight-year-old girl.

Because he was not yet aged 16, he escaped the death penalty and was sentenced to life imprisonment.

Released 20 years later on account of his 'exemplary behaviour' in prison, the then 35-year-old Jones returned to Abertillery, where he is believed to have visited the graves of his young victims.

By 1947 he was in London and, later settling in Fulham, married and had a daughter.

He died in 1971, but matters do not rest there, with his name having been linked in recent years to the mysterious killer dubbed 'Jack the Stripper', responsible for the murders of six prostitutes in London between 1964 and 1965.

Also known as 'the London nude murders', 'the Hammersmith nudes' or 'the Hammersmith murders', the naked bodies of his victims were found either dumped in the River Thames or in and around the city of London itself.

In common with the notorious nineteenth century Jack the Ripper, he has never been identified – although a number of theories as to his identity have been advanced over the years.

Among them is a claim by author Neil Milkins in his 2001 book *Who was Jack the Stripper?* that Harold Jones was the killer.

Other sources, however, stress that the author's evidence is circumstantial and that the *modus operandi* of the prostitutes' murders does not fit with the two murders that he did indeed commit when aged 15.

Chapter four:

On the world stage

Bearers of the proud name of Jones have excelled in a number of pursuits, not least in the world of entertainment.

From door-to-door vacuum cleaner salesman, builder's labourer and lorry driver to international star, **Tom Jones** is the Welsh singer who was born Thomas Jones Woodward in the small community of Pontypridd in 1941.

His first major hit was the 1965 *It's Not Unusual*, while in the same year he won a Grammy Award for Best New Artist.

A succession of hits have followed, including *Green Green Grass of Home*, from 1966, the 1968 *Delilah* and, from 1971, *She's a Lady*, while he received another major boost to his career in 1999 when the single *Sex Bomb* became his biggest hit to date.

His wife Melinda, better known as Linda and to whom he had been married for 59 years, died in 2016.

The entertainer, who received a BRIT Award for Outstanding Contribution to Music in 2003, has, at the time of writing, sold in excess of 100 million records.

The recipient of numerous awards, **Grace Jones** is the Jamaican-American singer, actress and model who was born Grace Mendoza in 1948 in Spanish Town, Jamaica.

Her top-selling albums include the 1977 *Portfolio* and the 2008 *Bulletproof Heart*, while films in which she has appeared include the 1985 *Conan the Destroyer* and the 1986 James Bond film, *A View to a Kill*.

Born in Chicago in 1933, **Quincy Jones** is the American conductor, record producer and film composer who, to date, has received no fewer than 79 Grammy Award nominations.

Jones, who worked as arranger for Frank Sinatra's 1964 *Swing* album, is also noted as producer of the late Michael Jackson albums *Thriller* and *Off the Wall*.

In the world of rock, **John Paul Jones** is the musician, songwriter and arranger who was born John Baldwin in 1946 in Sidcup, Kent.

Best known as the bassist and keyboardist for the British rock band Led Zeppelin, he now pursues a successful solo career as a musician and producer.

Born in Manchester in 1945, **Davy Jones** was the singer, songwriter and actor who is best known as having been the lead vocalist from 1965 to 1971 of the pop group The Monkees, enjoying hits that include *Daydream Believer* and *Last Train to Clarksville*.

He died in 2012, while in a different musical genre **Aled Jones** is the Welsh classical singer who was born in 1970 in Bangor.

Only fifteen years old when he recorded the best-selling *Walking in the Air*, the theme from the animated film *The Snowman*, he is also noted as a presenter of BBC TV's *Songs of Praise*.

Best known for her recording in 1964 of *Tainted Love*, a major hit in later decades for British band Soft Cell, **Gloria Jones** is the American singer and songwriter who was born in 1945 in Cincinnati.

She had been romantically involved with the British pop star Marc Bolan when, in September of 1977, the car she was driving was involved in a road accident that claimed Bolan's life.

Honoured by America's National Endowment for Arts in 1989 with its Jazz Masters Award, **Hank Jones** is the veteran jazz pianist and composer born in 1918 in Vicksburg, Mississippi, and who has played with such jazz greats as Ella Fitzgerald, Charlie Parker and Nancy Wilson.

Back to rock music, **Kenney Jones**, born in London in 1948, is the drummer who, after playing with the Small Faces in the 1960s, joined The Who in 1979 following the death of drummer Keith Moon.

Born in 1969 in Tredegar, Wales, **Nicholas Jones**, also known as Nicky Wire, is the bassist and lyricist with Welsh rock band Manic Street Preachers, while, also in Wales but in a different musical genre, **Paul Jones** is the leading international baritone who was born in Cardiff in 1974.

Born in 1942 in Portsmouth, **Paul Jones** is the English singer, actor and musician best known as the vocalist and harmonica player with the 1960s band Manfred Mann, while **Malcolm Jones**, born in Inverness in 1959, is a musician and songwriter with Scottish band Runrig.

Described as the greatest living country singer, **George Jones** was born in 1931 in Saratoga, Texas. Married to country singer Tammy Wynette, his many hits include the 1959 *White Lightning* and the 1983 *I Always Get Lucky With You*.

Also in the world of music, David Robert Hayward Jones was the musician, record producer, arranger and actor better known as **David Bowie**.

Born in 1947 in Brixton, London, by the time of his death in 2016 he had sold an estimated 136 million albums worldwide, including the 1969 *Space Oddity*, *The Rise and Fall of Ziggy Stardust and the Spiders from Mars*, from 1972, and the 2003 *Suburbia*.

Ranked among the ten best-selling acts in UK pop history and ranked 39th by *Rolling Stone* magazine in 2004 in its list of the 100 greatest rock artists of all time, he modestly declined a British knighthood in 2003.

His son, **Duncan Jones**, is the film director, producer and screenwriter born Duncan Zowie Hayward Jones in Beckenham, Kent, in 1971, and who directed the acclaimed 2009 *Moon*.

Married to American actor Michael Douglas in 2000 but separating from him in 2013, **Catherine Zeta-Jones** is the Welsh actress born in Swansea in 1969.

It was following roles in a number of British and American television productions that she came to international prominence in 1996 for her role in *The Phantom*, while her portrayal of Velma Kelly in the 2002 *Chicago* earned her a number of awards that include an Academy Award for Best Supporting Actress.

Born in 1946 in San Saba, Texas, **Tommy Lee Jones** is the American actor and film director whose film roles include the 1981 *The Executioner's Song* and the 1997 *Men in Black*, while he received an Academy Award nomination for Best Actor for the 2007 *In the Valley of Elah*, and an Academy Award for Best Supporting Actor in 1993 for the *The Fugitive*, starring beside Harrison Ford.

On the television screen, **Ruth Jones**, born in 1967 in Bridgend, Wales is the award-winning actress, comedian, singer and writer best known as one of the co-writers and stars of the popular comedy series *Gavin and Stacey*.

Born in London in 1970, **Rupert Penry-Jones** is the English actor best known for his role in the British television spy series *Spooks*, while **Terry Jones**, born in 1942 in Colwyn Bay, is the Welsh comedian, actor, author and screenwriter best known as a member of the former *Monty Python* television and film team.

Across the Atlantic, **James Earl Jones**, born in 1931 in Arkabutla, Mississippi, is the American actor and recipient of a 2009 Screen Actors Guild

Lifetime Achievement Award whose films include the 1989 *Field of Dreams*, the 1990 *The Hunt for Red October* and, from 1995, *Cry, the Beloved Country*.

Born in 1947 in Stoke-on-Trent, **Freddie Jones** is the English character actor whose many film roles include the 1970 *The Man Who Haunted Himself* and, from 2004, *Ladies in Lavender*, while **Griff Rhys Jones** is the Welsh comedian, writer and television presenter who was born in Cardiff in 1953.

Known for his 1980s' British television comedy series *Alas Smith and Jones*, along with fellow comedian the late Mel Smith, he is also a recipient of the 1994 Laurence Olivier Theatre Award for Best Comedy Performance, for his role in the play *Absolute Turkey*.

Behind the camera lens, **Michael Caton-Jones** is the Scottish film director whose credits include the 1989 *Scandal*, the 1990 *Memphis Belle* and, from 2006, *Basic Instinct 2*; born Michael Jones in Broxburn, West Lothian, in 1957, he added 'Caton' to his surname after his marriage to his first wife, Beverly Caton.

Combining film with football, **Vinnie Jones**, born in 1965 in Watford, is the former English midfielder who played for teams that include Wimbledon, Leeds and Chelsea and now pursues an equally successful career as an actor.

His best known film role is the 1998 *Lock, Stock and Two Smoking Barrels*, while others include the 2000 *Snatch* and, from 2009, *Year One*.

From film and football to the golf course, **Bobby Jones**, born in 1902 in Atlanta, Georgia, has been described as one of the greatest golfers to have ever competed at both national and international level.

By the time he decided to quit the game at the age of only 28, he had achieved the unique 'Grand Slam' of winning all four major golf tournaments – the amateur and open championships in the USA and Britain – in a single year (1930); he was inducted into the World Golf Hall of Fame three years after his death in 1971.

Combining rugby and athletics, **Ken Jones**, born in 1921 in Blaenavon, Monmouthshire was the Welsh international rugby union player who, as an athlete, won a silver medal in the 4x400-metres relay at the 1948 Olympics; he died in 2006.

Also on the athletics track, **Barbara Jones**, born in 1937, is the former American athlete who won a gold medal in the 4x100-metres at the 1952 Olympics and gold for the same event at the 1960 Olympics.

Bearers of the Jones name have also excelled in the creative world of literature.

Born in 1949 in Lexington, Virginia, **Gayl Jones** is the contemporary African American writer whose novels include the 1975 *Corregidora* and whose poetry includes the 1981 *Song for Anninho*, while Dennis Feltham Jones was a noted British science fiction writer.

Born in 1917 and better known as **D.F. Jones**, his futuristic 1966 novel *Colossus* was later filmed as *Colossus: The Forbin Project*, while his last novel, *Bound in Time*, was published in 1981, the year of his death.

Drawing his inspiration from harrowing personal experience as a soldier, **James Jones** was the American author best known for his novels based on the Second World War.

Born in 1921 in Robinson, Illinois, he enlisted in the U.S. Army in 1939 and witnessed the Japanese attack on Pearl Harbor two years later.

This led to his first novel, the 1951 *From Here to Eternity*, which was later filmed, as was his second novel, the 1962 *The Thin Red Line*; he died in 1977.

No account of the Jones' could perhaps be complete without a reference to one famous fictional bearer of the name.

Dressed in 'trademark' leather jacket and fedora, step forward the intrepid archaeologist Dr Henry Walton Jones, Jr; better known as **Indiana Jones**, or "Indy."

Played by Harrison Ford, he has been the action hero in a series of films that include the 1981 *Raiders of the Lost Ark*, the 1984 *Indiana Jones and the Temple of Doom*, the 1989 *Indiana Jones and the Last Crusade* and, from 2008, *Indiana Jones and the Kingdom of the Crystal Skull*.